IT'S OKAY TO HAVE AN OSTOMY

Ann Favreau

IT'S OKAY TO
HAVE AN OSTOMY

Ann Favreau

Prepared for printing by:
Personalized Press Publishing
Jean Airey
916 Suncrest Lane
Englewood, FL

DEDICATION

This book is dedicated to those who have or will have ostomy surgery in the hope that it will provide some knowledge, allay their fears, and inspire them to live life to the fullest.

ACKNOWLEDGEMENTS

I want to thank my husband Ray for his love and support throughout my ostomy journey.
The encouragement of my family and friends continues to sustain me. There are so many individuals who have been there along the way, it would be impossible to list them. However, I do want to recognize some special people who have passed on. They were instrumental in my initial healing and encouraged me to become involved in leadership in the local support group and then in the United Ostomy Association. Al Clark, Helen Geoffrion, and Florence Cohen were incredible mentors.

It's Okay To Have An Ostomy

THE ROSEBUD

I chose the rosebud for the cover because many
people refer to a stoma, the bright red opening on the
abdomen through which waste travels, as a rosebud.
It does look like a red rose of flesh. In the language of
flowers the red rose signifies love, respect, and
courage. These are the special things that an
ostomate requires to lead a fulfilling life.

In 1988 a teaspoon of blood, a diagnosis of colorectal cancer, and a sigmoid colostomy changed my life. In those early days dealing with pain and despair I was encouraged to write about my experiences by a professor who was a member of my local support group. Poetry was the genre that I used. Over the years I continued to express my feelings and shared my work with others. Many wrote to say my words resonated with them. I hope they have meaning for you.

THE TASK

He challenged me to share my voice,
And pen my thoughts for you.
Once asked, I simply had no choice.
I had to follow through.

The need to write my story down,
The act of self-reflection,
Is easier than speech unwound
And spoken introspection.

Though sharing was the main intent,
My path from pain to healing,
The process seemed to circumvent
To illuminate my feelings.

The words of verse that flowed from me
Revealed a startling goal,
That living with an ostomy
Can enrich my simple soul.

I hope my words will challenge you
To rise above the crowd,
And share your special story too,
Then shout with voice aloud
   WE ARE REBORN FROM THE ASHES OF DISEASE!

Ostomy surgery is a life-saving procedure that can result in so many changes. Our body image is different. We have to deal with altered plumbing and attachments on our skin to hold waste. Some years after this poem was published in the *Ostomy Quarterly*, I heard from a woman who said she placed a copy of it on her fridge and read it every morning to help her get through the day.

RECLAMATION

Illness, pain, and surgery.
I've been cut apart.
Left to cope with healing,
And sorrow in my heart.

But as my body starts to mend,
Self care becomes mundane,
A little voice within my soul
Murmurs this refrain...
You're alive!

Just like you, I had to learn a new vocabulary. Stoma was described as a piece of intestine, brought to the surface and turned back like a cuff.

A CUFF, A STOMA

A fold of fabric that heightens style,
A turning of tissue that lightens life.
A slap of harsh reality!

A crease of linen at ankle's edge,
A moistened membrane folded back,
A crimson belly blow!

A quiet collector of useless lint,
A vibrant seamless spillway,
A jab against finality!

Then there was the terminology for the waste containers. Some people called them appliances; others, pouches and then there was the generic term bags. Finding the right one that met my needs was facilitated by a talented Wound Ostomy Continence Nurse. I knew that an important part of me had been removed. However, because of the research and development of reliable products, I could live a productive life.

NORMALCY

No one knows she's an ostomate
With pouch beneath her dress.
She stands before an audience
That she will soon address.

No one knows he's an ostomate,
This young man in his teens,
Playing ball and having fun
In bathing suit or jeans.

Pouches give them confidence,
Light barriers from strife.
Plastic holds their secret
As they go on living life.

Many ostomy surgeries result from colitis, Crohn's Disease, birth defects, or trauma. Because mine resulted from colorectal cancer, the worry about a cancer diagnosis was uppermost in my mind.

CHALLENGING THE BULLIES

Cancer cells are bullies
Beating up my dreams,
Threatening my life force
At every turn, it seems.
Yet hope is the avenger,
And action is the key
Opening the cells of fear,
Slashing spirit free.
Challenging the bullies,
Taking back my dreams,
Living each and every day,
My soul light beams!

When you receive a cancer diagnosis, you not only have to deal with it yourself, but also explain what is happening to many others. It was very difficult to give the news to the principal of my school, fellow teachers, college students and let the children in my kindergarten classes know that I would be leaving school for the rest of the year. However, telling my family was the most painful process.

CANCER TALK

Fearfully I told my Mom of cancer's harsh invasion,
Acting brave and feigning nonchalance.
Mama said, "Just deal with it and then get on with life!"
But choked on unshed tears
 'Cause I'm her baby.

She never asked for details.
We'd just chat 'bout surface stuff,
While worry sat between us at the table.
I sugar coated terror and played the stoic part,
The delegated role
For Mama's baby.

My daughters, on the other hand,
Craved all the dire detail,
When cancer came a calling at my door.
On tables cleared for feelings,
Honest talk was frosting free.
Masking self was not an act
For Ma's granddaughters.

I still remember the words of the surgeon when I went back for my six-week check up.

"I took out all the cancer. You are not a victim. Get on with your life."

Those words were so affirming that I embraced each day with a new vitality. I have shared this poem with many at Relay for Life events. I was delighted when it was published in *Coping* magazine.

STEPPING OUT

Step out of the frame of fear, my dear
Though cancer fills your mind.
Step out of the frame of dread instead
And leave your cares behind.

Step out of the frame of helplessness
And see your options through.
Step out of the frame of hopelessness
And look at life anew.

Step out of the frames and stride away
From cancer's gripping strife.
Advance with hope for a better day
Step forward and on with life.

I was a cancer survivor. I didn't need chemo or radiation. I joined the ranks of women everywhere who lived with the hope that the disease would not reoccur. I was one of the fortunate ones. It has not.

SURVIVOR GIRLS

Survivor girls are young or old
But have a single common goal
To live each day with zeal.

We have a tumor big or small,
And join the ranks of spirits all
Who fight for life and feel
A bond with other women.

We share the struggle,
Feel the pain, as one by one
We do regain a sense of strength.

Tears of joy, tears of sorrow
Bond us in the female marrow
Of survivor flesh and bones.

Through sunny days and weary nights
We never, ever, lose the sight
Of our quest for quality life.

Before the surgery I had planned to go to Australia and New Zealand with a group of teachers to attend the International Reading Association Conference and visit schools. I had canceled the trip. Now with the doctor's permission, I was able to rejoin the group and three months later with a new colostomy I was on my way. As I packed my bag and plenty of supplies, I was eager to take my healing body to the other side of the world. I would fill the void of disease with images pulsating with life.

DRESS FOR LIFE

Step into those lacy panties of living.
Fill your bra with cups of courage.
Slip on a daring dress of dignity.
You're a survivor, girl
Flaunt it!

When I returned from abroad, I joined the Ostomy Association of Greater Springfield, Massachusetts. At their Sunday afternoon meetings I met wonderful people who helped me with the practical aspects of dealing with an ostomy. I found that as I reached out to help others, I was able to heal myself.

PASSAGE

Telling, sharing, feeling, caring,
All are active actions on the pathway to healing,
Stepping stones to living with an ostomy.

Calling, reaching, helping, teaching,
Extends the thoroughfare of life to others
That we meet along the way.

Laughing, crying, loving, sighing,
Line the avenue of faces
There to lift us o'er the potholes of despair.

Destination normalcy is not a static passage,
But a jagged journey resolutely trekked.

At the support group meetings everyone was encouraged to tell his story. When people asked how you were doing, they expected an honest response. There were no pretenses here. It didn't matter if you were a new ostomate or an experienced one that developed new issues; someone was there to offer support. I recall the day a burly, tattooed man arrived on a noisy motorcycle with his wife clinging to his back.

STRENGTH

Motorcycle man, burly and strong,
Holds his wife's hand gently,
As she tells her painful tale to those
Who listen so intently.

He's brought her here from far away,
For help that he can't give.
Disease has wracked her solid frame.
He's thankful she will live.

As chapter members offer aid,
Her tears begin to flow.
His mighty arm encircles her.
Oh, he loves her so!

She gathers strength from those who know
All that she's been through.
He's thankful they have made the trip.
She'll heal and he will too.

I soon learned that everyone had good and bad days. A leak, skin rash, an embarrassing moment, a bout of feeling sorry for yourself was all part of the recovery process. It became apparent to me that humor and hope were the assets that got people through the trying times. My feelings mirrored those of others, and that was comforting. The members of this group, ostomates, spouses and caregivers, enhanced the support I took for granted from my loving husband, family and friends.

HOPE

Hope is like a yellow balloon
With its string of optimism
Threaded through my fingers.
Close to my soul when I'm feeling okay,
Strung out of reach on difficult days.

Pulling, tugging on my spirit,
It floats higher and higher out of sight.
I worry that the prick of depression
Will burst the orb,
Spilling the helium of healing,
Leaving me with the limp string.

But this balloon is blown with faith,
Tied with family love.
Though tossed and turned by the tempest,
I yank it in, this sphere of hope
Helping me endure.

Because I was an educator and a lifelong learner, I took the opportunity to seek out information about the different kinds of ostomies, diet and care regimens, social and advocacy issues relating to these conditions. The *Ostomy Quarterly* and subsequently *The Phoenix* magazines were wonderful resources. Printed materials from the United Ostomy Association and the manufacturers of ostomy equipment added to my knowledge. However, attending my first UOA national convention was amazing. In the sessions I learned current information and was able to view new products in the exhibit hall. At that time I could not have foreseen that I would visit the offices of the major manufacturers as a leader of this national organization and have the opportunity to see firsthand the rigorous testing and research development that goes into making ostomy products reliable and discreet. I attended many conferences and met people who would become lasting friends. The variety of ages, children to elders, surprised me and I was pleased to discover that folks could live a long life with an ostomy. As we interacted together, listened to motivational speakers, and socialized, I observed the change in many from fear to acceptance. At one event I met a young singer who went through this transformation.

OSTOMY HARMONY

I went to sing my ostomy songs
And make them laugh
And shed a tear,
Without a clue that
They were there for me.

Around the pool the scars on skin
Healed the ones I had within.
Others shared their tunes with me
The lyric of a family.

I went to spread a little cheer
And stayed to face my unsung fear.
Their songs became a melody
That comforted the inner me.

I went to sing my special songs
And make them laugh
And shed a tear.
Now I know my soul will say
They were there for me.

As a UOA trained visitor, I sat by many a bedside, talked to people on the phone, and now by email continue to connect with others to offer encouragement. I suggest the resources found at the United Ostomy Associations of America website ostomy.org. One of my early visiting experiences was with a woman who had multiple sclerosis, had just lost her husband and was facing ostomy surgery. How does one offer comfort in such a situation?

TWO VISITS

She sits in a wheelchair sobbing.
MS has her body,
Grief has her soul.
Her mind is fraught with doubts.

I hold her hand and listen.
Surgery is imminent.
Death stole her spouse.
Will the pouch give her freedom?

I stay by her side an hour.
Speak quiet words.
Offer my support.
Her spirit seems to calm.
****

She sits in the hospital smiling.
Healing has begun.
The pouch is friend, indeed.
Family love will move her on.

Traveling with an ostomy seems to be an issue for some ostomates. Not me, I have been all over the world. My modes of transportation have included the usual- planes, trains, autos, busses and boats. However, I have also experienced rickshaws, tuk tuks, pedicabs, funiculars, trams, cable cars, a dragon boat, sampan, ferries, water taxis, felucca, gondola, and even a camel ride.

Toileting in various parts of the world can be a challenge but also quite an experience. I have been in a huge bathroom in a former raja's palace in India and in a small shack with a porcelain covered hole in the ground. I've even had to empty a pouch in a field sheltered by a large umbrella and on a rocking boat through a hole in the wooden floor. Finding the flushing mechanism can take an astute sense of observation. Sometimes they are located on the toilet, but in many areas of the world you may find a lever on the floor to step on or a pull chain attached to an overhead tank. In rural areas it can simply be a pail of water. I have changed pouches in opulent bathrooms and in places with no running water. Being prepared for any encounter has given me a sense of control. Having an ostomy won't keep me from meeting people of other cultures, finding wonder in the ordinary and marveling at the awesome wonders of the world.

WINDOW EYES

Window eyes
View with awe
The wonders of the world.

Pyramids, Eiffel Tower,
Great Wall, Three Gorges Dam,
Petra, Luxor, Taj Mahal

Superb constructions
Wrought by man.

Window eyes
See without judging
The people of the world.

Chinese fishermen
Egyptian craftsmen
Indian washerwomen

French bakers
Japanese calligraphers
Aborigine wanderers

Guatemalan farmers
Australian herders
Italian vintners

Common people
Living uncommon lives.

Window eyes
Look upon the world.

Marvel at the awesome,
Find wonder in the ordinary.

In my leadership roles with the United Ostomy Association I met ostomates from all over the country and found that they, too, were providing assistance in their local communities. Now, as Secretary of the International Ostomy Association, I have become aware of the needs of ostomates around the globe. I started this journey in a local support group in Massachusetts and now facilitate one in Florida. I have come full circle.

THE HEALING CIRCLE

Caring people
Conquer affliction
Move as survivors
To comfort others.

Listening ears
Empathetic hearts
Hands outreached
To make a difference.

Touching others
Links of care
Connect us all
In the Healing Circle

On a recent Mediterranean Cruise, a ninety- year- old gentleman asked me if I had any regrets about my life. My answer surprised him and me. I replied that I could have regretted having colorectal cancer that resulted in a colostomy, but the experience has enriched my life. I have journeyed from cancer to caring. Along the way I have been an educator, traveled the world, published prose and poetry about my experiences and met wonderful people. Perhaps I have had a positive influence on some of them by demonstrating that it's okay to have an ostomy.

OSTOMATES

Ordinary people
With life saving surgery
Coping with change

Fearful at first
Hopeful at last
Helping others

Displaying self-confidence
Concealing impairment
Sharing a voice.

It's Okay to Have an Ostomy

RESOURCES

United Ostomy Associations of America, Inc. (UOAA): www.ostomy.org 1 800 826-0826
>   Ostomy information and a list of affiliated support groups in the United States

The Phoenix magazine: www.phoenixuoaa.org
Official publication of UOAA
P.O. Box 3605, Mission Viejo, CA 92690
>   Current ostomy and research information, stories about ostomates

International Ostomy Association (IOA): www.ostomyinternational.org
>   Regional contacts for Europe, the Americas, Asia, and the South Pacific

Ostomy Association of Canada: www.ostomycanada.ca
>   Ostomy information and a list of Canadian chapters

Wound Ostomy Continence Nurses Society (WOCN): www.wocn.org 888 224-9626

MANUFACTURERS OF OSTOMY SUPPLIES

Have nurses who answer telephone questions
Coloplast: www.coloplast.com   888 726-7872
Convatec: www.Convatec.com 800 422-8811
Hollister: www.hollister.com   888 740-8999
Nu Hope: www.nu-hope.com   800 899-5017

FURTHER READING

Ann Favreau:
   Window Eyes
   www.amazon.com
   People and Places
   favra1@comcast.net

Brenda Elsagher:
   If the Battle is Over, Why am I Still in Uniform?
   I'd Like to Buy a Bowel Please! Bedpan Banter
   It's in the Bag and Under the Covers
   www.amazon.com

Carol Larson:
   Positive Options for Colorectal Cancer
   Hunter House Publishers, P.O. Box 2914, Alameda,
   CA 945010-0914
   When the Trip Changes
   Weathering the Storm
   www.Bookmobile.com, www.amazon.com

Elizabeth and Phillip Prosser:
   Unwanted Baggage
   www.amazon.com

It's Okay To Have An Ostomy

ABOUT THE AUTHOR

Ann Favreau is a retired educator who had a colostomy in 1988. She was President of the Ostomy Association of Greater Springfield, MA and then went on to hold offices in the national organization, the United Ostomy Association, serving as President in 2000 – 2002. She was appointed Secretary of the International Ostomy Association in 2005 and is currently Secretary of the Coordination Committee of IOA and a member of the National Colorectal Cancer Roundtable. Ann lives in Venice, FL with her husband Raymond and facilitates the Venice Ostomy Support Group, an affiliate of the United Ostomy Associations of America.

Ann and husband Ray on one of their trips.

It's Okay To Have An Ostomy

Made in the USA
Middletown, DE
24 January 2022